DATE DUE

FEB 1999

CHJ

BC-3

CRACKING THE WALL
The Struggles of the Little Rock Nine

CRACKING THE WALL

The Struggles of the Little Rock Nine

by Eileen Lucas
illustrated by Mark Anthony

Carolrhoda Books, Inc./Minneapolis

To the Little Rock Nine, and to the children of all races in schools across America, who prove that the walls that keep people apart are wrong. I especially dedicate this book to the students of Morgan Park High School in Chicago, where I learned this lesson. —E. L.

Text copyright © 1997 by Eileen Lucas
Illustrations copyright © 1997 by Mark Anthony

This book is available in two editions:
Library binding by Carolrhoda Books, Inc.
Soft cover by First Avenue Editions
c/o The Lerner Publishing Group
241 First Avenue North, Minneapolis, MN 55401 U.S.A.

Library of Congress Catologing-in Publication Data

Lucas, Eileen.
    Cracking the wall : the struggles of the Little Rock Nine /
by Eileen Lucas ; illustrated by Mark Anthony.
        p.   cm. — (Carolrhoda on my own books)
    Summary: A brief introduction to the nine African-American students who integrated Central High School in Little Rock, Arkansas, in 1957.
    ISBN 0-87614-990-5 (lib. bdg.)
    ISBN 1-57505-227-X (pbk.)
    1. School integration—Arkansas—Little Rock—History—
20th century—Juvenile literature. 2. Afro-American students—
Arkansas—Little Rock—History—20th century—Juvenile
literature. 3. Central High School (Little Rock, Ark.)—
History—Juvenile literature. 4. Little Rock (Ark.)—Race
relations—Juvenile literature. [1. School integration—
Arkansas—History. 2. Afro-Americans—Civil rights—History.
3. Arkansas—Race relations.] I. Anthony, Mark, 1962– ill. II.
Title. III. Series: Carolrhoda on my own book.
LC214.23.L56L83 1997
379.2'63'0976773—dc21   96-45003

Manufactured in the United States of America
1 2 3 4 5 6 – SP – 02 01 00 99 98 97

Author's Note

Not too long ago, laws kept black and white Americans apart in many places. This was called segregation. There were "white only" waiting rooms and drinking fountains, buses and hotels. "Colored only" signs directed black people to smaller, dirtier places. There were separate schools for white children and for black children. The ones for black children were almost always older and smaller. They had to use the books that schools for white children didn't want anymore.

In 1954, the Supreme Court of the United States said that segregated schools were wrong. Children could not be kept apart and denied a good education just because of the color of their skin.

In 1957, in Little Rock, Arkansas, nine black students were chosen to move from the high school for black children to the high school for whites, Central High. They became known as the Little Rock Nine. This is their story.

A car drove slowly down a quiet street
in Little Rock, Arkansas.
When the driver saw the house
he was looking for, he slowed even more.

It was the home of L. C. and Daisy Bates.
They owned an African-American
newspaper in the city.
Suddenly, someone inside the car
threw a rock.
It crashed through the front window
of the Bates home.

The sound of shattering glass
was followed by dogs barking
and babies crying.
And by the sound of the men in the car
laughing as they sped away.
Inside the house, no one was laughing.
The rock had almost hit Daisy Bates
as she sat on the couch.
She looked at the glass on the floor.
She knew that the people who threw
the rock wanted to scare her.
They wanted her to stop helping
the black students who would be going
to Central High.
But she was not scared.
She was going to help those students
and end segregation,
laws that kept blacks and whites apart.

Central High was huge.

It sat on a whole city block all by itself.

It had five floors of classrooms
and more than two thousand students.

Now nine of them would be black.

One of them was Ernest Green.
This would be his last year of high school.
He wanted to graduate from Central
and go to college.

Six of the other students were in
eleventh grade.
Minnijean Brown was lots of fun.
She liked to make people laugh.
She also liked to sing.

Terrance Roberts was cheerful and smart.
He could always think of things to say
to make people smile.
Elizabeth Eckford liked to sew.
While waiting for school to start,
she made a new dress to wear.

Thelma Mothershed was small and thin
and had a weak heart.
But she had a strong mind.
Gloria Ray spoke quietly
of things that were important to her.

Melba Pattillo was pretty
and did well at lots of things.
She knew that there were
"five floors of opportunities"
waiting at Central.

Jefferson Thomas and Carlotta Walls
were in tenth grade.
Jeff had been one of the fastest runners
at his old school.
Carlotta was on the student council.

All nine students were well behaved
and hardworking.
They were all excited about
going to Central High.
They knew that they would not
be allowed to join
the school's teams and clubs.
Minnijean could not sing in the glee club.
Jeff could not join the track team.
Ernest could not play his sax in the band.
The black students could only go to class.
"But even that will be something,"
Ernest encouraged the others.

Many white Southerners
did not want to see an end to segregation.
They did not want to see black children
in school with white children.
Some of them went to talk to
Orval Faubus, the governor of Arkansas,
about it.

On Labor Day,

Governor Faubus spoke on radio and TV.

He said that soldiers were standing

outside Central High.

He also said that the black students

should not go to Central High.

"He's stirring up trouble,"

said Melba's grandmother.

Melba's grandmother was right.

The next morning,

a crowd of people gathered

at Central High.

Soldiers with helmets and guns

stood silently around the building.

They looked like they were ready for war.

Would there be a battle at Central High?

Only white students
went to Central that day.
The black students stayed home.
They did not want trouble.
But they did want an education.
And Central High was supposed to be
their school too.

Late that night,
Mrs. Bates called all the students
except Elizabeth.
Her family did not have a phone.
Mrs. Bates would try
to reach her the next day.
She told the others
to meet in the morning
a few blocks from Central.

Then they would walk to school together.

On Wednesday morning,

seven of the nine students met

as planned.

Two ministers walked

in front of them.

One was white, one was black.

Two more walked behind.

As the group drew near the school,
they saw the crowd of people.
The faces that glared at them
were full of anger and hate.
People shouted at them
and called them names.
But the students kept on walking.

When the students reached the soldiers,
they were told to go home.
They were told that they could not
go into the school.
Sadly, they turned around and left.

Melba Pattillo had not even made it
to the meeting place.
She and her mother had been
chased away by angry white men.
They had to return home.

Things were even worse
for Elizabeth Eckford.
She never got the message
about where to meet the others.
After praying with her family,
she rode a bus to school by herself.
When she got off the bus, all she could see
was the angry crowd.
Then she saw the soldiers
standing by the school.
She thought they would protect her.

As Elizabeth walked toward them,
someone squirted ink on her dress.
A woman screamed in her face.
Elizabeth tried to ignore the angry voices.
She tried not to show
how frightened she was.

Finally she reached the soldiers.
Instead of letting her past,
they blocked her way.
They pointed their guns at her.
They were not on her side.

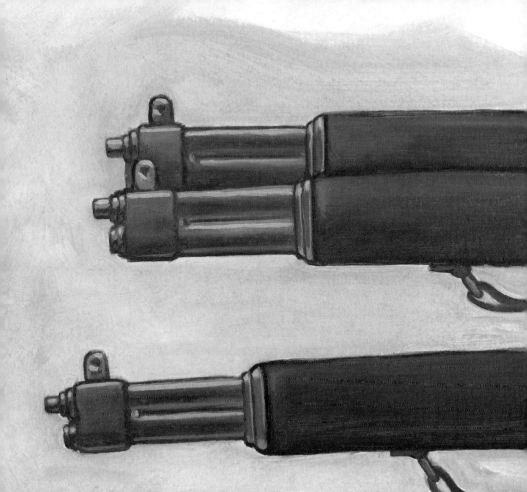

Behind her sunglasses,
Elizabeth's eyes filled with tears.
She turned and walked away.
People in the crowd pressed close.
Someone shouted, "Get her!"

Elizabeth saw a bus stop
down the street.
She made it there and
sat down on a bench.
A kind man sat next to her.
"Don't let them see you cry,"
he whispered.
When the bus came,
a woman stepped forward to help.
She rode with Elizabeth
to where her mother worked.

For three weeks,
the soldiers and the angry crowd
kept the black students out
of Central High.
The students had to do their schoolwork
at Daisy Bates's house.
It would have been easy for them to quit
and go back to their old schools.
But they knew that
what they were doing was right.

34

Then one day the soldiers left.

"What will happen next?"

asked Elizabeth.

"Get ready for school," said Mrs. Bates.

As usual, a crowd of people waited
by the front doors of Central High.
Policemen directed the black students
to a side door where the crowd
could not see them.

Inside, people helped the students find their classrooms.

Thelma did not feel well.

Someone took her to the office.

But she did not want to go home.

She had waited too long to get in.

"I'm not giving up now," she said.

When the crowd found out that
the black students were inside,
they grew very angry.
They beat up some reporters
who were outside.
The students could hear the shouts
as they sat in their classrooms.

The police chief was afraid that
more people would be hurt.
He asked the black students to leave.
In a garage under the school,
they got into police cars.
"Get down and stay down,"
the chief told the students.
"Don't stop for anything,"
he told the drivers.
The cars sped away.
For a few hours, the black students
had been in Central High.
But they had not been allowed to stay.

News programs all around the country
talked about what was happening
in Little Rock.
Many Americans were angry about it.
They sent letters to the students,
inviting them to come to school
in their towns.

The president of the United States,
Dwight Eisenhower,
was angry too.
No crowd could keep American children
out of school, he said.
He sent a new group of soldiers
to Little Rock.
Their job would be to let
the black students into Central High.

The next day, the United States Army
arrived in Little Rock.

On Wednesday morning, soldiers knocked
on Mrs. Bates's front door.

"We're ready for the students," they said.

That day the nine students rode to school
in an army car.
There were soldiers
in helicopters overhead.
There were soldiers everywhere.
They marched with Ernest
and Elizabeth and the others
up the front steps of the school.
Minnijean said it made her feel
like an American.
Ernest said it gave him a "big feeling."

The Little Rock Nine walked
right through the front doors
of Central High.
Melba later said that at that moment,
"The whole nation took
one giant step forward."

45

Front row: Thelma Mothershed, Elizabeth Eckford, Melba Pattillo.
Back row: Jefferson Thomas, Ernest Green, Minnijean Brown,
Carlotta Walls, Terrance Roberts, Gloria Ray

Afterword

For a while, soldiers went with the Little Rock
Nine to all their classes. Most of the students were
either nice to them or didn't pay much attention to
them. But there were a few who were still angry
that the black students were there, and they were
very mean.

After a few months, most of the soldiers left, and
things got even worse. The troublemakers called
the black students names. They dumped food on
them at lunchtime. They threw pencils at them.
They kicked them and knocked their books down.

Finally graduation day came. Ernest Green became

the first black student to graduate from Central High. Later he said, "I knew that I had accomplished what I'd come there for. I had cracked the wall."

That wall was the wall of segregation, the wall that kept black people and white people apart. Ernest Green and the eight other students helped crack the wall by showing that black people and white people *could* go to school together.

But Governor Faubus still did not think it was right. He closed all the public high schools in Little Rock for the 1958–59 school year rather than let black and white students be together. Black *and* white students had to find other ways to get their education. Melba spent her last year of school in California, and Minnijean went to New York. When the Little Rock schools reopened in fall 1959, Carlotta and Terrance returned to Central High School. The others went back to their old schools. All of them graduated and went on to college and successful careers.

In 1987, the Little Rock Nine returned to visit Central High. This time, the crowd that greeted them cheered them as heroes. The president of the student body was a young black man. The mayor of Little Rock was a black woman.

The Little Rock Nine helped to crack the wall. Now it is up to each of us to continue to tear down the walls that keep people apart.

Important Dates

May 17, 1954—The U.S. Supreme Court declares that segregated schools are unconstitutional.

Summer 1957—Seventeen students are selected to move from all-black schools to Central High. By August, the list is narrowed to nine.

September 2, 1957 (Labor Day)—Governor Faubus places soldiers around Central High.

September 3, 1957—The black students are asked to stay home on the first day of school.

September 4, 1957—The black students are turned away as they try to enter Central High.

September 23, 1957—The black students enter Central by a side door, but police take them home, fearing for their safety.

September 24, 1957—U.S. Army troops arrive in Little Rock.

September 25, 1957—The Little Rock Nine enter Central High through the front doors, accompanied by U.S. troops.

May 27, 1958—Ernest Green graduates from Central High.